*This Book Is a*

*B.H. Publishing LLC*

*Presentation*

DAVID CLIFTON KING

# NAVIGATING LOVE

# &

# ADHD

# A GUIDE FOR

# PARTNERS

## For Your Information

The content provided in this book is intended for general informational purposes only. It is not a substitute for professional medical advice, diagnosis, or treatment. The author of this book is not a licensed medical practitioner. While the author believes in the veracity of the content presented herein, it should not be considered professional medical advice.

Readers are reminded to consult with qualified healthcare professionals for medical advice tailored to their individual circumstances. The author makes no representations or warranties regarding the accuracy, completeness, or suitability of the information provided. Therefore, any reliance on the information within this book is at the risk of the reader.

Individuals with specific medical conditions or concerns should always seek the guidance of a qualified healthcare professional. The author encourages readers to exercise their own judgment and seek professional advice when needed.

*No part of this publication may be reproduced, stored or transmitted in any form or by any means, electronic, mechanical, photocopying, recording, scanning, or otherwise without written permission from the publisher. It is illegal to copy this book, post it to a website, or distribute it by any other means without permission.*

B.H. Publishing LLC ©2024  All Rights Reserved

*For Cecilia*

*My most grateful appreciation and gratitude to my life partner for her inspiration, encouragement, technical assistance, and patience..*

*—David Clifton King*

# Preface

In the labyrinth of love, every twist and turn presents a new set of challenges. For more than twenty years, your author traversed a daunting, complex maze alongside my partner, attempting to navigate highs and lows, triumphs and setbacks and seemingly unattainable expectations of a close connection.

Little did I realize that hidden within the complexities of our often stressful relationship was a very crucial unrecognized piece of the puzzle. It was my partner's previously diagnosed condition: Attention Deficit Hyperactivity Disorder (ADHD).

She had actually disclosed her ADHD diagnosis in a casual conversation long before our marriage. Regrettably, I was clueless about ADHD and how it would play a role in our life journey. I did not resonate with her important revelation, perhaps even wondering if she might be exaggerating.

It would be much later, before I could come to terms with the thought that it was my failure to understand her very different, unique way of thinking that was causing stress on our relationship. My discovery would call for prompt action. So, fueled by the hope of finally establishing a more intimately close connection and armed only with lots of hindsight and the lightbulb that had gone on in my aging brain, I began the arduous task of educating myself about ADHD.

. After much reading about ADHD, I came to the conclusion that much of our partnership's frustrations and stress were possibly connected to my inability to comprehend my partner's uniquely different thought patterns.

As I studied, I happily began to realize that the knowledge I was gaining in the research process was turning out to be a genuine epiphany. As I read about the symptoms and the impact of ADHD on relationships, it seemed as if the text had been written specifically for our partnership. This inspired positivity and the belief that a solution was close at hand.

*Navigating Love and ADHD: A Guide for Partners* is written with the heartfelt hope that sharing this experience and research will benefit others undergoing similar circumstances and lead to a magnificent positive outcome.

It is my hope that this guide will also serve as a realization to folks that it is never too late to embark on a positive journey to refresh and renew your mindset and to restore peace and healing to a cherished love partnership.

**—David Clifton King**

# Table of Contents

**Chapter One** ............................................................. 9
**Finding Out About ADHD**

**Chapter Two** ............................................................ 12
**The ADHD Brain Structure**

**Chapter Three** ......................................................... 15
**ADHD in Adults**

**Chapter Four** ........................................................... 18
**Navigating Love & ADHD in Partnership**

**Chapter Five** ............................................................ 23
**Strategies for Improving Communication**

**Chapter Six** .............................................................. 26
**Creating A Balanced Playing Field**

**Chapter Seven** ......................................................... 29
**Navigating the Journey Together**

**Chapter Eight** .......................................................... 32
**Strengthening Your Partnership**

**Chapter Nine** ........................................................... 36
**Signs of Positivity**

**ADHD Research References** ............................. 38-39

# Chapter One
## Finding Out About ADHD

### What is ADHD?

ADHD stands for Attention Deficit Hyperactivity Disorder. It is a neurodevelopmental disorder characterized by difficulties with attention, hyperactivity, and impulsivity.

ADHD is typically classified into three subtypes: predominantly inattentive type, predominantly hyperactive-impulsive type and combined type, which involves both inattention and hyperactivity-impulsivity.

### Common Symptoms Associated with ADHD

*Inattention:* Difficulty sustaining attention, easily distracted, difficulty organizing tasks, forgetfulness, frequent careless mistakes, etc.

*Hyperactivity*: Fidgeting, restlessness, excessive talking, difficulty staying seated, constant movement etc.

*Impulsivity:* Impulsive decision-making, difficulty waiting for one's turn, interrupting others, acting without considering consequences etc.

*Variability:* Variability can vary greatly from person to person and may appear differently depending on age and other factors.

### What ADHD is NOT
### Common Myths

**Myth One:** ADHD is not a real disorder; it is an excuse for bad behavior.

ADHD is a recognized neurodevelopmental disorder with a substantial body of scientific research supporting its existence. Neuro imaging studies have shown differences in brain structure and function in individuals with ADHD compared to those without it. Additionally, genetic studies have identified specific genes associated with ADHD, further supporting its biological basis.

**Myth Two:** ADHD only affects children. Adults cannot have ADHD.

While ADHD is often diagnosed in childhood, it can persist into adulthood for many years. Research suggests that around 60-70% of children diagnosed with ADHD continue to experience symptoms into adulthood. Additionally, ADHD can often be under-diagnosed in adults, as symptoms may manifest differently or be mistaken for other conditions.

**Myth Three:** ADHD is caused by bad parenting or too much social media or television screen time.

While parenting styles and environmental factors definitely can influence behavior, ADHD is primarily a neurobiological disorder with strong genetic components. Studies have shown that ADHD tends to run in families, and genetic factors account for a significant portion of the risk for developing ADHD. While screen time and other environmental factors may exacerbate symptoms, they are not the underlying cause of ADHD.

**Myth Four:** People with ADHD need to try harder to focus and pay attention.

ADHD is characterized by impairments in executive functioning, which include difficulties with attention, impulse control, and working memory. These challenges are not simply a matter of willpower or effort; they are rooted in differences in brain functioning. While strategies like behavior therapy and medication can help manage symptoms, they may not completely eliminate them.

**Myth Five:** Medication is the only effective treatment for ADHD.

While medication can be an effective treatment for ADHD symptoms, it is not the only option. Behavioral interventions, such as cognitive behavioral therapy (CBT) and psychoeducation, can also be helpful, especially when combined with medication. Lifestyle changes, such as exercise, proper nutrition and organization strategies, can also contribute to symptom management. By addressing these myths with evidence-based information, we can promote a better understanding of ADHD and support individuals affected by it.

## How is ADHD Diagnosed?

Diagnosis typically involves a comprehensive evaluation by a healthcare professional, such as a psychiatrist or psychologist. The diagnostic criteria for ADHD are outlined in the *Diagnostic and Statistical Manual of Mental Disorders (DSM-5)*, published by the American Psychiatric Association.

Gathering information from the individual, as well as parents, teachers, or other significant individuals regarding the individual's behavior and symptoms is also part of the diagnostic process as is the utilization of standardized tools to assess ADHD symptoms and their impact on daily functioning.

Differential diagnosis is used in ruling out other potential explanations for the symptoms, such as learning disabilities, anxiety disorders, or mood disorders.

# Chapter Two

## The ADHD Brain Structure

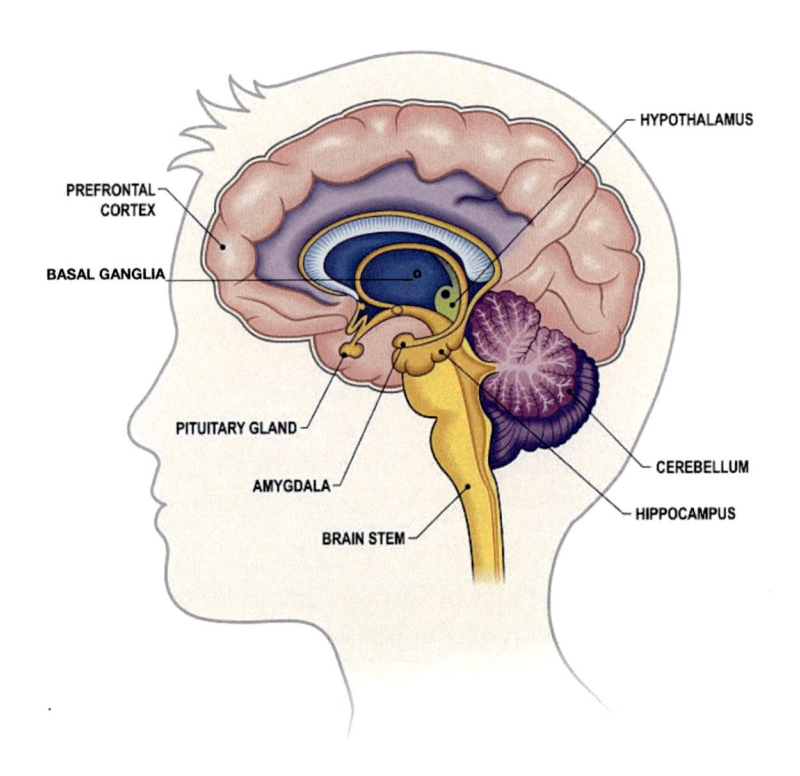

*Activity in the prefrontal cortex and the basal ganglia is connected to ADHD.*

# ADHD Brain Structure and Function

The Prefrontal Cortex (PFC) is responsible for decision-making, impulse control and attention regulation. It tends to show structural and functional differences in individuals with ADHD. These variances often result in difficulties with inhibition, planning, and sustained attention.

The Basal Ganglia region of the brain is involved in motor control and plays a role in regulating attention and impulsivity. Differences in the basal ganglia structure and function have been observed in those with ADHD, potentially contributing to hyperactivity and impulsive behaviors.

Connectivity between the prefrontal cortex and basal ganglia, known as the frontostriatal circuit, is also implicated in ADHD. Dysfunction within this circuitry can lead to impairments in executive functions, such as working memory and cognitive flexibility.

Neurotransmitters such as dopamine are associated with motivation, reward, and attention. Dysregulation of dopamine transmission is thought to be a key factor in ADHD, contributing to difficulties in sustaining attention and regulating impulses.

Norepinephrine plays a role in arousal, alertness, and the fight-or-flight response. Irregularities in norepinephrine levels or receptor sensitivity may be contributors to the hyperactivity and impulsivity observed in ADHD Although traditionally associated with mood regulation, serotonin also modulates attention, impulse control and executive functions. Alterations in serotonin levels or function can contribute to ADHD symptoms, particularly in regulating mood swings and behavior.

## Attention, Impulse Control and Executive Function

Individuals with ADHD often struggle with maintaining attention on tasks that are not inherently stimulating or rewarding. They may exhibit symptoms of inattention, such as being easily distracted, forgetful, or being prone to making careless mistakes.

Impulsivity is a hallmark feature of ADHD, characterized by acting without forethought, difficulty delaying gratification and interrupting others. This lack of impulse control can lead to social and academic challenges.

Executive functions encompass a range of cognitive processes, including planning, organization, working memory and cognitive flexibility. In some instances, ADHD can impair these functions, leading to difficulties in goal-oriented behavior, time management and problem-solving.

Understanding the neurobiological underpinnings of ADHD can inform interventions and treatments aimed at addressing the specific challenges faced by individuals with this condition. Additionally, recognizing the multifaceted nature of ADHD can help mitigate stigma and promote empathy and support for those affected.

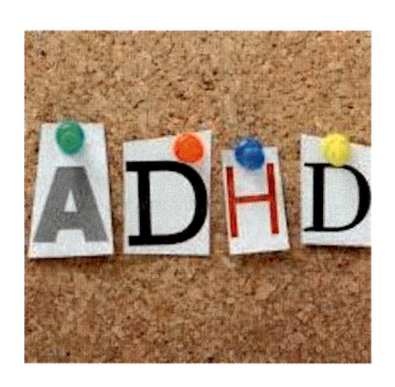

# Chapter Three
## ADHD and Adults

**A**ttention Deficit Hyperactivity Disorder is not just confined to childhood. It is found in adulthood, though it might manifest differently. The prevalence of ADHD in adults varies across studies and populations, but it is estimated that around 5% of adults worldwide have ADHD. However, due to misdiagnosis, the actual numbers may even be higher.

*Time Management and Organization:* Adults with ADHD often struggle with time management, organization and planning tasks effectively. They may find it challenging to prioritize and complete tasks on time.

*Decision Making and Impulsivity:* Impulsivity can lead to difficulties in decision-making and controlling behaviors. This could manifest in impulsive spending, risky behaviors, or speaking without thinking.

***Attention and Focus:*** Difficulty sustaining attention and focus can affect performance at work or in academic settings. Adults with ADHD may find it hard to concentrate during meetings, lectures, or while reading.

***Emotional Dysregulation:*** Emotional dysregulation is common, leading to mood swings, irritability and difficulty managing stress. This can strain relationships and impact overall well-being.

***Procrastination:*** Adults with ADHD often struggle with procrastination, putting off tasks until the last minute due to difficulty initiating or maintaining focus.

## Symptoms Often Vary

Remember to keep in mind that the characteristic symptoms of ADHD can be very different with different individuals. The condition affects individuals of all intellectual levels, including those with high IQs and glowing accomplishments.

The impact of ADHD extends beyond symptom presentation and severity to encompass factors such as age, gender, coexisting conditions and individual strengths and weaknesses.

For instance, children with ADHD may demonstrate different symptom patterns compared to adults, with hyperactivity often being more prominent in childhood and giving way to more subtle signs of inattention in adulthood. Gender differences also play a role, with boys more commonly diagnosed with ADHD than girls, though girls may exhibit different symptoms, such as internalizing behaviors, leading to underdiagnosis or misdiagnosis.

Coexisting conditions, such as anxiety, depression, learning disabilities, or executive function deficits, can further influence the manifestation of ADHD symptoms and complicate diagnosis and treatment. Additionally, individual strengths, such as creativity, adaptability, and hyperfocus, can coexist alongside ADHD symptoms, shaping an individual's unique profile and response to interventions. Understanding the diverse ways in which ADHD can manifest among different individuals is crucial for accurate diagnosis, personalized treatment planning, and effective support strategies.

*Academic and Occupational Difficulties:* ADHD can lead to underachievement in academic or professional settings. Difficulties with focus, organization and time management may result in poor performance or frequent job changes. However, my special ADHD partner, quite conversely was an honor student in high school and college and an accomplished over achiever who retired from a highly successful teaching career of 27 years without negative incident.

*Relationship Strain:* Challenges in communication, emotional regulation and impulsivity strain relationships with partners, as well as family and friends. This can definitely lead to conflicts and cause feelings of inadequacy and incompatibility.

*Mental Health Issues:* Untreated ADHD is associated with a high risk of developing other mental health conditions, such as depression, anxiety and substance abuse disorders.

*Financial Problems:* Impulsivity and poor decision-making can lead to financial difficulties, including debt mismanagement and overspending.

*Legal Issues:* Impulsivity and risk-taking behaviors may sometimes increase the likelihood of legal problems such as speeding tickets, accidents, or legal conflicts.

Early diagnosis and appropriate treatment, including therapy and medication, when necessary, can significantly improve the quality of life for adults with ADHD. It cannot be overstated that it is essential for individuals experiencing symptoms to seek evaluation and support from healthcare professionals.

# Chapter Four
## Navigating Love and ADHD in Partnership

Attention Deficit Hyperactivity Disorder can significantly negatively impact personal relationships and particularly within the context of love partnerships. The challenges faced by couples where one partner has ADHD are multifaceted and can harm the relationship in many different ways.

***Impact on Personal Relationships.*** Individuals with ADHD may struggle with organization, time management and impulsivity, which lead to frustration and misunderstandings with their partner. Additionally, symptoms such as forgetfulness procrastination and distractibility can make it difficult to follow through on commitments and responsibilities within the relationship. However, it must be noted that this is not always the case. ADHD can be structured in various ways depending on genetic influence, childhood experience, trauma and other factors.

## The Partner ADHD Copes with Challenges

***Difficulty with Focus and Attention:*** Individuals with ADHD may struggle to maintain focus on tasks, leading to unfinished projects and difficulty following conversations or instructions. But again, not always.

***Impulsivity:*** Impulsive behaviors such as interrupting others, making hasty decisions, or engaging in risky activities can strain relationships and lead to misunderstandings.

***Time Management Issues:*** Difficulty with time perception and organization can sometimes result in chronic lateness, missed deadlines and a sense of being overwhelmed.

***Forgetfulness:*** Forgetfulness related to appointments, responsibilities and obligations can lead to frustration for both the individual and those around them.

***Emotional Irregularity:*** Intense emotions, mood swings and difficulty managing frustration can impact daily functioning and create a presumptive feeling of incompatibility by both partners.

***Hyperactivity:*** Some individuals with ADHD experience hyperactivity, which can manifest as restlessness and difficulty sitting still. This condition often makes it difficult to relax and fully engage in intimate moments.

***Struggles with Executive Functioning:*** Challenges with planning, prioritizing tasks and initiating and sustaining activities can sometimes hinder productivity and success in various areas of life.

***Difficulty with Structure and Routine:*** Individuals with ADHD may resist or struggle with maintaining routines and structure. Or they may take an opposite path and attempt to schedule everything into an overly structured routine.

All of this said, personal experience indicates to me that certain positive thinking individuals like my partner have the ability to not consciously suffer with their ADHD condition. But it also reinforces my conclusion that, although many of the symptoms may be obvious, ADHD affects different individuals quite uniquely.

# Navigation Difficulties for the Non-ADHD Partner

Until the non-ADHD partner understands the ADHD condition and learns how to respond to it, he or she is impacted negatively in many ways. One of the most difficult impacts may very well be the constant, ongoing challenge of searching for a much-needed closer emotional connection and the helplessness and feelings of emotional distance caused by its absence.

***Frustrations and Misunderstandings:*** Partners may become frustrated and feel misunderstood when the symptoms of ADHD lead to communication breakdowns over unfulfilled expectations.

***Feelings of Being Overwhelmed:*** Supporting a partner with ADHD can feel extremely overwhelming, especially when trying to juggle additional responsibilities while coping with negativity and feelings of partner incompatibility.

***Concern for the Partner's Well-being:*** The partner may worry a lot about the loved one's general well-being, particularly regarding the issues like impulsivity, forgetfulness, mood swings and emotional walls of separation that seem impenetrable.

***Strain on Relationship Dynamics:*** The challenges associated with ADHD can definitely strain the dynamics of the relationship and lead to increased tension, resentment or even hurtful words accentuating feelings of imbalance and negativity.

***Need for Patience and Understanding:*** The partner must particularly work around their own shortcomings and focus on cultivating patience and understanding in order to navigate the ups and downs of living with ADHD, including maintaining positive support during setbacks and disappointments.

***Balancing Support vs. Independence:*** Finding the right balance between providing support and encouraging independence is challenging for the partner, as they must navigate to best support their loved one without enabling or becoming overly controlling.

***Educating Both Partners About ADHD:*** Both partners should consider reading about ADHD to better understand each other's state of mind and to help in organizing effective strategies for improving communication.

***Acceptance:*** The non-ADHD partner must be able to summon a large portion of patience and hold it in place in order to create and maintain the necessary mindset of acceptance. Practicing the art of acceptance can be a very demanding task.

***Mismatched and Unrealized Expectations:*** The non-ADHD partner may often have expectations regarding communication and planning that are not aligned with the abilities and tendencies of the partner with ADHD.

***Emotional Distress:*** The inconsistency and impulsivity associated with ADHD can lead to both emotional and physical exhaustion for both partners. The non-ADHD partner may feel neglected or frustrated, while the partner with ADHD may experience guilt or shame over their difficulties.

***Role Strain:*** The responsibilities of managing household tasks, finances and childcare may sometimes fall disproportionately on either partner, leading to feelings of resentment and imbalance in the relationship.

***Communication Breakdowns:*** ADHD symptoms such as forgetfulness and impulsivity can contribute to communication breakdowns and misunderstandings. Important discussions may be derailed or forgotten, leading to conflict and stress.

Effective communication is essential in any relationship, but it is particularly challenging when one partner has ADHD.

## Communication Breakdowns May Include

***Difficulty Listening:*** The partner with ADHD often struggles to maintain focus during conversations, leading to misunderstandings and incorrect interpretations of the partner's words.

***Impulsivity:*** The Impulsivity factor can lead to interruptions and speaking out of turn, making it difficult for both partners to express themselves fully and feel like they are being heard.

***Forgetfulness:*** Forgetfulness can result in important conversations or agreements being overlooked or forgotten, causing frustration and creating resentment between partners.

***Emotional Dysregulation:*** ADHD symptoms can contribute to emotional dysregulation, which is the abnormality or impairment in the regulation of a metabolic, physiological, or psychological processes. This makes it extremely challenging for both partners to engage in productive and empathetic communication during conflicts or disagreements.

Navigating the impact of ADHD partnership requires much patience and understanding. Partners need to create effective communication strategies, carefully designed for the unique, individual needs of the couple.

Your author wholeheartedly recommends seeking professional support, such as couples therapy or ADHD coaching, this can be extremely helpful in addressing the challenges of strengthening the relationship.

# Chapter Five
## Strategies for Improving Communication

Living with Attention Deficit Hyperactivity Disorder (ADHD) can present immense challenges for both partners regarding communication.

However, with the right strategies, couples can rekindle understanding, and empathy and restore a lost intimate connection to their relationship.

### Effective Communication Techniques

***Active Listening and Validation:*** Practice active listening. Encourage each other to listen attentively without interruption. Reflect back on what the other person is saying to ensure understanding.

***Validate Feelings:*** ADHD symptoms are frustrating for both partners. So, validate each other's emotions and experiences without judgment. Acknowledge the challenges and the efforts that are being made to overcome them.

***Set Realistic Expectations and Boundaries:*** Work on clearly defining responsibilities and expectations within the relationship. Break tasks into manageable steps to prevent overwhelm.

***Establish Boundaries to Protect Each Other's Well-Being:*** Communicate openly about personal needs and about the limitations related to ADHD symptoms.

***Use Non-Verbal Communication Cues:*** Pay attention to body language. Non-verbal cues can convey a lot of information. Be mindful of each other's body language to help better understand underlying emotions and intentions.

***Use Visual Cues:*** Visual reminders and cues can be helpful for both partners. Utilize visual aids such as calendars, to-do lists, or color-coded schedules to enhance communication and organization.

## Developing Coping Strategies Together

***Collaborate On Solutions:*** Work together to identify effective coping strategies for managing ADHD symptoms. Experiment with techniques such as mindfulness, time management techniques, or organization systems.

***Regular Check Ins:*** Schedule regular check-ins to assess what communication strategies are working and which ones need adjustment. Adapt and refine your approach based on ongoing experience and partner feedback.

***Never Play the Blame Game:*** Don't ever play the blame game, even when your partner's words or actions might seem to pull you into a conflict. Blaming each other to prove your point launches arguments that may ultimately end in an exchange of harsh words and destructive consequences.

Exchanges about whose fault it is will always escalate into arguments, even when your point may possibly be well taken. Find a much mellower way to approach the issue without finding fault.

By implementing these communication strategies, couples can strengthen their bond, navigate the challenges related to ADHD and cultivate a supportive and understanding relationship environment. Remember, communication is a skill that requires practice and patience, but it will significantly enhance your relationship and create precious harmony.

## Seek Professional Help Together

***Do Not Fear Seeking Professional Support.*** Consider seeking therapy or counseling from a professional who specializes in ADHD and relationships. A therapist can help provide personalized strategies and support tailored to your unique needs as a couple.

Educate yourselves about ADHD and its impact on relationships. Attend workshops, read books, or join support groups to gain insights. Learn effective communication techniques from professionals.

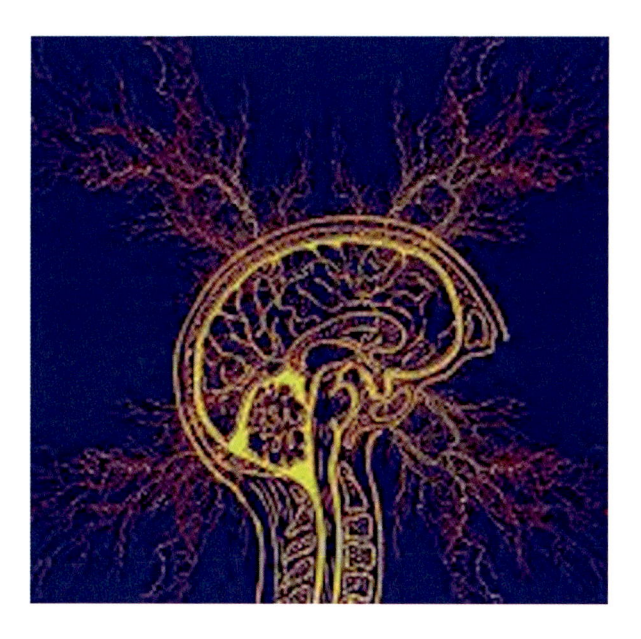

***Listen when your partner speaks!***

# Chapter Six
## Creating A Balanced Playing Field

In this chapter, we will explore strategies for managing partnership balance by way of integrating routines for adding structure, organization and time management and by minimizing distractions to improve focus.

### Stay Aware of Each Other's Needs

Living with ADHD as a couple can present unique challenges. By working together and implementing effective strategies, you can navigate these challenges and strengthen your relationship.

*Prioritize Tasks:* Break down tasks into smaller, manageable steps and prioritize them based on urgency and importance. Focus on completing one task at a time to avoid feeling overwhelmed.

*Open Communication:* Establish open and honest communication about how ADHD symptoms impact both partners. Encourage each other to share frustrations, concerns, and successes.

*Education:* Learn about ADHD together. Understanding the symptoms and how they manifest can help foster empathy and reduce misunderstandings.

*Shared Responsibilities:* Divide tasks and responsibilities based on each partner's strengths and interests. Consider creating a list of household tasks and their requirements and decide together who will take on each responsibility.

## Create Routines and Structure

*Consistent Schedule:* Establish a consistent daily routine and stick to it as much as possible. Set regular times for waking up, meals, work, and relaxation.

*Visual Timelines:* Use visual aids such as calendars, planners, or whiteboards to display schedules and upcoming events. This helps both partners to maintain the necessary mindset.

*Decluttering*: Maintain an organized living space by decluttering regularly. Designate specific areas for commonly misplaced items like keys, wallets, and phones. If you happen to be even a small-scale hoarder, declutter as soon as it is practical!

*Time Blocking:* Allocate specific blocks of time for different activities throughout the day. Use timers or alarms to stay on track and transition between tasks smoothly.

*Utilize Technology:* Explore apps and tools designed to aid with organization and time management. These could include task managers, reminder apps, or digital calendars that sync across devices.

## Minimize Distractions to Improve Focus

*Designated Workspace:* Create a designated workspace free from distractions where you can focus on tasks without interruption. This could be a separate room or a quiet corner of your home.

*Limit Screen Time:* Set boundaries around screen time, especially during important tasks or quality time together. Consider using apps or browser extensions to block distracting websites or notifications. This will have to be done with painstaking caution, considering today's addictive distractions.

***Mindfulness and Meditation:*** Practice mindfulness techniques or meditation to improve focus and reduce impulsivity. Even a few minutes of deep breathing or guided meditation can help calm the mind and increase attention span.

By implementing these strategies together as a couple, you can effectively manage ADHD symptoms, create a supportive environment and strengthen your relationship. Remember to be patient with yourselves and each other as you navigate this crucial part of the journey together.

***Some days things seem to get out of hand.***

# Chapter Seven
## Navigating the Journey Together

In this chapter, we will explore practical tips and techniques for couples to navigate ADHD symptoms together, focusing on creating routines, organization, and time management. Additionally, we will discuss the importance of teamwork and mutual support in implementing these strategies most effectively.

You are fully aware, by now, that navigating the journey of love and ADHD presents variable challenges for both individuals and for couples. However, with the proper strategies and support system, it is very possible to effectively manage symptoms and cultivate a more fulfilling relationship.

### Strategies for Managing the Symptoms

Establishing routines and implementing organizational strategies can provide structure and stability, which are essential tools for managing ADHD symptoms.

***Set Regular Daily Routines:*** Create consistent daily routines for tasks such as waking up, mealtimes, work or study periods and bedtime. Having a predictable schedule can help reduce impulsivity and increase productivity.

***Utilize Visual Tools:*** Use visual aids such as calendars, planners and to-do lists to help organize tasks and responsibilities. Consider using color-coding or digital tools that sync across devices for added convenience.

**Designate Specific Spaces:** Designate specific areas in your home for different activities, such as work/study areas, relaxation zones and organization stations. Keep these spaces clutter-free and conducive to focus.

**Break Tasks into Manageable Steps:** Break down large tasks into smaller, more manageable steps. Encourage each other to focus on completing one step at a time. Celebrate achievements along the way!

***Minimize Distractions and Improve Focus:*** *ADHD often involves major difficulties with attention and focus, but there are strategies couples can employ to minimize distractions and enhance concentration.*

**Create Distraction Free Zones:** Identify and eliminate sources of distraction in your environment, such as turning off notifications on electronic devices and minimizing background noise during focused tasks.

## Implement Intelligent Time Management

**Techniques:** Find out how to use techniques like the Pomodoro Technique, which involves working in short bursts followed by brief breaks, to maintain focus and improve productivity.

**Practice Mindfulness and Meditation:** Incorporate mindfulness practices into your daily routine to help calm the mind and improve attentional control. Consider practicing mindfulness exercises together to support each other's efforts.

**Encourage Physical Activity:** Regular exercise has been shown to improve focus and concentration in individuals with ADHD. Engage in physical activities together, such as walking, jogging, or practicing yoga, to boost cognitive function.

**Teamwork and Mutual Support**: Effective management of ADHD symptoms requires teamwork and mutual support within the relationship.

## How Couples Support Each Other

**Communicate Openly and Honestly:** Foster open communication about ADHD-related challenges, goals, and strategies. Be willing to listen non-judgmentally and offer support and encouragement to each other.

**Divide Responsibilities Fairly:** Recognize each other's strengths and weaknesses when dividing household and relationship responsibilities. Work together to create a balanced and manageable division of tasks.

**Provide Positive Reinforcement:** Acknowledge and celebrate each other's accomplishments, no matter how small. Positive reinforcement can help motivate continued effort and progress.

**Seek Professional Help When Needed:** Don't hesitate to seek support from healthcare professionals, therapists, or ADHD coaches if you are struggling to manage symptoms effectively. Professional guidance can provide valuable tools and strategies tailored to your unique needs as a couple.

Managing ADHD symptoms as a couple requires patience, understanding, and collaboration. By creating routines, minimizing distractions and offering mutual support, couples can navigate the challenges of together while strengthening their bond.

Remember that progress may be gradual, but with perseverance and teamwork, you are cultivating a fulfilling and harmonious relationship, despite the challenges.

# Chapter Eight

## Strengthening Your Partnership

## Steps to Strengthen Your Partnership

Build resilience and trust in your partnership: Building resilience and trust in your relationship involves fostering open communication, practicing empathy and working through complex challenges together. Resilience is built through overcoming obstacles as a team, while respect and trust grow, as the partners consistently demonstrate reliability, honesty and support for each other.

Look for joy and connection despite ADHD challenges: For couples facing ADHD challenges, it is important to focus on understanding the condition, developing coping strategies and finding activities that foster connection and enjoyment. This might involve setting clear expectations, creating structured routines and engaging in shared interests to maintain a strong bond despite the challenges.

***Celebrate successes and milestones together:*** Celebrating successes and milestones strengthens the bond between partners. By acknowledging and appreciating each other's accomplishments, both big and small, the positive mindset is constantly reinforced. It is an opportunity to express gratitude, support and admiration for each other's efforts, creates a positive and encouraging working atmosphere in the relationship.

***Seek outside support and resources:*** Often, couples require additional support to navigate challenges or enhance their relationship. This could involve seeking guidance from therapists, counselors, or support groups to learn effective communication strategies. This will help partners gain insight into relationship dynamics and access resources tailored to their specific needs.

Seeking outside support demonstrates a positive commitment to the relationship's growth and well-being. It might very well offer information that will strengthen your commitment.

*The ADHD partner and the non-ADHD partner share difficult, yet different challenges.*

# Chapter Nine

## Signs of Positivity

In the preceding chapters, we have explored and restated the impact on the dynamics of love that occurs when a partnership is grappling with ADHD.

In the process, we have learned that the condition brings with it difficult, complex challenges not only for the person with the condition, but amazingly difficult challenges for the other partner as well.

The substantial personal observations your writer has made regarding the navigation of love with ADHD and the additional research done has convinced me that following the important affirmations below should be necessary and very helpful in your journey. I believe them to be universally applicable.

By faithfully practicing and placing them as high priorities added to your renewed mindset, you will be equipping yourself with the positivity that will help you safely navigate your journey through love with the presence of the complex challenges of ADHD.

### Reflect on Your Journey

Take a moment and reflect on your journey thus far, both past and present and future. Recall the initial uncertainties, the frustrations, fears and self-doubts that once clouded your path. Let your partner know often when they do or say something that makes you happy. Then, take a moment to celebrate the positive.

Embrace the quirks and idiosyncrasies that make your relationship special. It is these very qualities that enrich the tapestry of your love connection.

Celebrate your victories, no matter how small and draw strength from the blessings of love and support that bind you together.

Share some time remembering moments of clarity, the small victories and the positive connections that affirm your bond. Your journey together is uniquely yours, with moments of joy, laughter and positive experiences.

Every triumph, no matter how seemingly small and insignificant, has contributed positivity to the collective development of your partnership.

## Positivity and Acceptance

While navigating the minefields of love with ADHD, maintaining a positive outlook becomes paramount. Practice your commitment to learning acceptance. It is very easy to become ensnared in a destructive cycle of negativity as you focus on the complexities and challenges at hand. However, re-framing your mindset and celebrating each other's strengths, triumphs and blessings, will cultivate an environment of optimism and mutual respect.

Remember, you are allies, not adversaries. You are 'dearest ones', united in a mutual commitment of support.

## Powerful Tools: Patience and Empathy

Patience and empathy are the major cornerstones of a thriving relationship. Recognize that ADHD manifests differently in each individual and that progress may probably be gradual.

Embrace your renewed mindsets of compassion and acceptance, seeking to understand rather than to judge. By fostering an environment of patience and empathy, you will create space for an open dialogue, and growth and healing will follow.

## Clear Communication Is Your Lifeline

Effective communication lies at the heart of all successful relationships. Poor communication builds inaccurate perception. Inaccurate perception clouds the intended solution and allows the journey to remain difficult.

Take the time to communicate openly and honestly with one another, expressing your needs, fears and aspirations. Practice active listening, seeking to understand your partner's perspective without interruption or judgment.

Remember, communication is not just about words but also about gestures, expressions, body language and actions.

By making a sincere effort to understand the challenges facing both partners and by focusing on the discovery of effective strategies, you are setting sail to embark on a successful journey. The attention paid to clear communication that you have shown will pay generous future dividends.

As we approach the conclusion of this guide, it is essential to recognize that even though ADHD presents many uniquely different hurdles, it must NOT be allowed to define the entirety of the relationship.

With willpower, patience, understanding, acceptance and extra special concerted effort, couples can not only weather the storms, but thrive in the radiant warmth of love's embrace. Newly found emotional intimacy naturally develops and becomes a reality when mutual respect is shown by both partners and each recognizes the sincere efforts being made to create happiness.

## Smile, Embrace Love and Life

As you journey upon the threshold of the future, be safe! Enjoy envisioning the awesome possibilities that lie ahead. As your skills develop, you will have the power to conquer adversity and forge a deeper connection with your partner. You will have begun the process of laying a solid foundation for a lifetime of renewed love and intimate partnership. Don't rush the voyage. Embrace the journey with an open heart and a steadfast resolve, knowing that with real love and patience and understanding, anything is possible.

As you travel your renewal path together, keep in mind that real love knows no bounds. With dedication and perseverance, you can traverse the distance that has kept you apart.

Embrace each other fully, celebrate your strengths and cherish the bond that unites you. At the finish line, it is love that sustains us, love that guides us and it is love that illuminates our paths forward. Thus far, you have become painfully aware that navigating love with ADHD is difficult, complex, and presents immense challenges.

Most importantly, you know now that navigating love and ADHD offers magnificent rewards. Imagine the joy you both will feel when the walls blocking the intimate connection you have sought for so long are finally torn away!

I bid a fond farewell to both partners as you travel your special journey. May your entire voyage be filled with boundless love, endless joy and recognition of the infinite positive possibilities!

—-David Clifton King

# ADHD Research References

*Attention Deficit Hyperactivity Disorder: A Handbook for Diagnosis and Treatment* by Russell A. Barkley.

*ADHD: Clinical Practice Guideline for the Diagnosis, Evaluation, and Treatment of Attention-Deficit/Hyperactivity Disorder in Children and Adolescents* by American Academy of Pediatrics.

*Attention Deficit Disorder: The Unfocused Mind in Children and Adults* by Thomas E. Brown.

*Taking Charge of ADHD: The Complete, Authoritative Guide for Parents* by Russell A. Barkley and Christine M. Benton.

*ADHD in Adults: What the Science Says* by Russell A. Barkley.

*Executive Functions: What They Are, How They Work, and Why They Evolved* by Russell A. Barkley.

*ADHD and the Nature of Self-Control* by Russell A. Barkley

*Attention Deficit Disorder: Diagnosis and Treatment from Infancy to Adulthood* by Edwin H. Kessler and Demitri Papolos.

*Driven to Distraction: Recognizing and Coping with Attention Deficit Disorder from Childhood Through Adulthood* by Edward M. Hallowell and John J. Ratey

*Taking Charge of Adult ADHD* by Russell A. Barkley

*The ADHD Effect on Marriage: Understand and Rebuild Your Relationship in Six Steps* by Melissa Orlov

# Additional References

**Children and Adults with Attention-Deficit/Hyperactivity Disorder (CHADD): CHADD** is a nonprofit organization dedicated to providing support and advocacy for individuals with ADHD and their families. Their website offers educational resources, support groups, and information on ADHD-related topics. Website: https://chadd.org/

**ADDitude Magazine:** ADDitude is a trusted source of information and support for individuals living with ADHD and related conditions. Their website features articles, webinars, expert advice, and community forums covering various aspects of ADHD. Website: https://www.additudemag.com/

**National Institute of Mental Health (NIMH) ADHD** https://www.nimh.nih.gov/health/topics/attention-deficit-hyperactivity-disorder-adhd/index.shtml

These websites offer reliable information and resources for understanding ADHD, its symptoms, diagnosis, treatment options, and strategies for managing the condition.

Made in the USA
Las Vegas, NV
04 May 2025